My Invention or Idea Book

A great way to capture and document your own original ideas!

By Joshua R. Embry

Use the following pages to document your ideas.
You can use this book for fun or for getting ready to patent your idea!

If you decide that you want to patent some or all of your ideas, the United States Patent and Trademark Office has a number or resources online.

As of the publication of this book, you can get great information here:
https://www.uspto.gov/patents-getting-started/general-information-concerning-patents

If that link is no longer valid when you read this book, try shortening the address to simply www.uspto.gov and follow their prompts following the word Patent until you find what you need.

Whether you're getting this for your creative 5 year old, or yourself, you'll love looking back over your ideas in years to come.

Ever say "I thought of that 10 years ago," well, prove it by documenting your ideas.

One of the most important parts of getting a patent for any idea or invention is to clearly document it from the start. This book will help start that process. The goal of this book is to allow you a clear and concise way to log the basics of your invention. You'll likely want to expand upon these ideas in further detail and further documentation. Use this book to answer basic questions you will need to address before getting your own patent. If you run out of pages, remember to order another book, then you can store your inventions in an organized way. Each new book will be a new volume of your inventions!

As always, if taking the next step and moving forward with a patent, seek advice from the USPTO as listed above and/or legal counsel.

Invention or Idea #: _____

Person who invented this: _____ Date: _____

What am I calling/naming it?

What does it do? (Describe what it does in 1-2 sentences):

How does it help someone or make something easier? (1-2 sentences)

Sketches: (If applicable, try to cover multiple angles or show movement)

Figure 1	Figure 2
Figure 3	Figure 4

Is this really worth making? Yes/No
What are my next steps?

Invention or Idea #: _____

Person who invented this: _____ Date: _____

What am I calling/naming it?

What does it do? (Describe what it does in 1-2 sentences):

How does it help someone or make something easier? (1-2 sentences)

Sketches: (If applicable, try to cover multiple angles or show movement)

Figure 1	Figure 2
Figure 3	Figure 4

Is this really worth making? Yes/No
What are my next steps?

Invention or Idea #: _____

Person who invented this: _____ Date: _____

What am I calling/naming it?

What does it do? (Describe what it does in 1-2 sentences):

How does it help someone or make something easier? (1-2 sentences)

Sketches: (If applicable, try to cover multiple angles or show movement)

Figure 1	Figure 2
Figure 3	Figure 4

Is this really worth making? Yes/No
What are my next steps?

Invention or Idea #: _____

Person who invented this: _____ Date: _____

What am I calling/naming it?

What does it do? (Describe what it does in 1-2 sentences):

How does it help someone or make something easier? (1-2 sentences)

Sketches: (If applicable, try to cover multiple angles or show movement)

Figure 1	Figure 2
Figure 3	Figure 4

Is this really worth making? Yes/No
What are my next steps?

Invention or Idea #: _____

Person who invented this: _____ Date: _____

What am I calling/naming it?

What does it do? (Describe what it does in 1-2 sentences):

How does it help someone or make something easier? (1-2 sentences)

Sketches: (If applicable, try to cover multiple angles or show movement)

Figure 1	Figure 2
Figure 3	Figure 4

Is this really worth making? Yes/No
What are my next steps?

Invention or Idea #: _____

Person who invented this: _____ Date: _____

What am I calling/naming it?

What does it do? (Describe what it does in 1-2 sentences):

How does it help someone or make something easier? (1-2 sentences)

Sketches: (If applicable, try to cover multiple angles or show movement)

Figure 1	Figure 2
Figure 3	Figure 4

Is this really worth making? Yes/No
What are my next steps?

Invention or Idea #: _____

Person who invented this: _____ Date: _____

What am I calling/naming it?

What does it do? (Describe what it does in 1-2 sentences):

How does it help someone or make something easier? (1-2 sentences)

Sketches: (If applicable, try to cover multiple angles or show movement)

Figure 1	Figure 2
Figure 3	Figure 4

Is this really worth making? Yes/No
What are my next steps?

Invention or Idea #: _____

Person who invented this: _____ Date: _____

What am I calling/naming it?

What does it do? (Describe what it does in 1-2 sentences):

How does it help someone or make something easier? (1-2 sentences)

Sketches: (If applicable, try to cover multiple angles or show movement)

Figure 1	Figure 2
Figure 3	Figure 4

Is this really worth making? Yes/No
What are my next steps?

Invention or Idea #: _____

Person who invented this: _____ Date: _____

What am I calling/naming it?

What does it do? (Describe what it does in 1-2 sentences):

How does it help someone or make something easier? (1-2 sentences)

Sketches: (If applicable, try to cover multiple angles or show movement)

Figure 1	Figure 2
Figure 3	**Figure 4**

Is this really worth making? Yes/No
What are my next steps?

Invention or Idea #: _____

Person who invented this: _____ Date: _____

What am I calling/naming it?

What does it do? (Describe what it does in 1-2 sentences):

How does it help someone or make something easier? (1-2 sentences)

Sketches: (If applicable, try to cover multiple angles or show movement)

Figure 1	Figure 2
Figure 3	Figure 4

Is this really worth making? Yes/No
What are my next steps?

Invention or Idea #: _____

Person who invented this: _____ Date: _____

What am I calling/naming it?

What does it do? (Describe what it does in 1-2 sentences):

How does it help someone or make something easier? (1-2 sentences)

Sketches: (If applicable, try to cover multiple angles or show movement)

Figure 1	Figure 2
Figure 3	Figure 4

Is this really worth making? Yes/No
What are my next steps?

Invention or Idea #: _____

Person who invented this: _____ Date: _____

What am I calling/naming it?

What does it do? (Describe what it does in 1-2 sentences):

How does it help someone or make something easier? (1-2 sentences)

Sketches: (If applicable, try to cover multiple angles or show movement)

Figure 1	Figure 2
Figure 3	**Figure 4**

Is this really worth making? Yes/No
What are my next steps?

Invention or Idea #: _____

Person who invented this: _____ Date: _____

What am I calling/naming it?

What does it do? (Describe what it does in 1-2 sentences):

How does it help someone or make something easier? (1-2 sentences)

Sketches: (If applicable, try to cover multiple angles or show movement)

Figure 1	Figure 2
Figure 3	Figure 4

Is this really worth making? Yes/No
What are my next steps?

Invention or Idea #: _____

Person who invented this: _____ Date: _____

What am I calling/naming it?

What does it do? (Describe what it does in 1-2 sentences):

How does it help someone or make something easier? (1-2 sentences)

Sketches: (If applicable, try to cover multiple angles or show movement)

Figure 1	Figure 2
Figure 3	Figure 4

Is this really worth making? Yes/No
What are my next steps?

Invention or Idea #: _____

Person who invented this: _____ Date: _____

What am I calling/naming it?

What does it do? (Describe what it does in 1-2 sentences):

How does it help someone or make something easier? (1-2 sentences)

Sketches: (If applicable, try to cover multiple angles or show movement)

Figure 1	Figure 2
Figure 3	Figure 4

Is this really worth making? Yes/No
What are my next steps?

Invention or Idea #: _____

Person who invented this: _____ Date: _____

What am I calling/naming it?

What does it do? (Describe what it does in 1-2 sentences):

How does it help someone or make something easier? (1-2 sentences)

Sketches: (If applicable, try to cover multiple angles or show movement)

Figure 1	Figure 2
Figure 3	Figure 4

Is this really worth making? Yes/No
What are my next steps?

Invention or Idea #: _____

Person who invented this: _____ Date: _____

What am I calling/naming it?

What does it do? (Describe what it does in 1-2 sentences):

How does it help someone or make something easier? (1-2 sentences)

Sketches: (If applicable, try to cover multiple angles or show movement)

Figure 1	Figure 2
Figure 3	Figure 4

Is this really worth making? Yes/No
What are my next steps?

Invention or Idea #: _____

Person who invented this: _____ Date: _____

What am I calling/naming it?

What does it do? (Describe what it does in 1-2 sentences):

How does it help someone or make something easier? (1-2 sentences)

Sketches: (If applicable, try to cover multiple angles or show movement)

Figure 1	Figure 2
Figure 3	Figure 4

Is this really worth making? Yes/No
What are my next steps?

Invention or Idea #: _____

Person who invented this: _____ Date: _____

What am I calling/naming it?

What does it do? (Describe what it does in 1-2 sentences):

How does it help someone or make something easier? (1-2 sentences)

Sketches: (If applicable, try to cover multiple angles or show movement)

Figure 1	Figure 2
Figure 3	Figure 4

Is this really worth making? Yes/No
What are my next steps?

Invention or Idea #: _____

Person who invented this: _____ Date: _____

What am I calling/naming it?

What does it do? (Describe what it does in 1-2 sentences):

How does it help someone or make something easier? (1-2 sentences)

Sketches: (If applicable, try to cover multiple angles or show movement)

Figure 1	Figure 2
Figure 3	Figure 4

Is this really worth making? Yes/No
What are my next steps?

Invention or Idea #: _____

Person who invented this: _____ Date: _____

What am I calling/naming it?

What does it do? (Describe what it does in 1-2 sentences):

How does it help someone or make something easier? (1-2 sentences)

Sketches: (If applicable, try to cover multiple angles or show movement)

Figure 1	Figure 2
Figure 3	Figure 4

Is this really worth making? Yes/No
What are my next steps?

Invention or Idea #: _____

Person who invented this: _____ Date: _____

What am I calling/naming it?

What does it do? (Describe what it does in 1-2 sentences):

How does it help someone or make something easier? (1-2 sentences)

Sketches: (If applicable, try to cover multiple angles or show movement)

Figure 1	Figure 2
Figure 3	Figure 4

Is this really worth making? Yes/No
What are my next steps?

Invention or Idea #: _____

Person who invented this: _____ Date: _____

What am I calling/naming it?

What does it do? (Describe what it does in 1-2 sentences):

How does it help someone or make something easier? (1-2 sentences)

Sketches: (If applicable, try to cover multiple angles or show movement)

Figure 1	Figure 2
Figure 3	Figure 4

Is this really worth making? Yes/No
What are my next steps?

Invention or Idea #: _____

Person who invented this: _____ Date: _____

What am I calling/naming it?

What does it do? (Describe what it does in 1-2 sentences):

How does it help someone or make something easier? (1-2 sentences)

Sketches: (If applicable, try to cover multiple angles or show movement)

Figure 1	Figure 2
Figure 3	Figure 4

Is this really worth making? Yes/No
What are my next steps?

Invention or Idea #: _____

Person who invented this: _____ Date: _____

What am I calling/naming it?

What does it do? (Describe what it does in 1-2 sentences):

How does it help someone or make something easier? (1-2 sentences)

Sketches: (If applicable, try to cover multiple angles or show movement)

Figure 1	Figure 2
Figure 3	**Figure 4**

Is this really worth making? Yes/No
What are my next steps?

Invention or Idea #: _____

Person who invented this: _____ Date: _____

What am I calling/naming it?

What does it do? (Describe what it does in 1-2 sentences):

How does it help someone or make something easier? (1-2 sentences)

Sketches: (If applicable, try to cover multiple angles or show movement)

Figure 1	Figure 2
Figure 3	Figure 4

Is this really worth making? Yes/No
What are my next steps?

Invention or Idea #: _____

Person who invented this: _____ Date: _____

What am I calling/naming it?

What does it do? (Describe what it does in 1-2 sentences):

How does it help someone or make something easier? (1-2 sentences)

Sketches: (If applicable, try to cover multiple angles or show movement)

Figure 1	Figure 2
Figure 3	Figure 4

Is this really worth making? Yes/No
What are my next steps?

Invention or Idea #: _____

Person who invented this: _____ Date: _____

What am I calling/naming it?

What does it do? (Describe what it does in 1-2 sentences):

How does it help someone or make something easier? (1-2 sentences)

Sketches: (If applicable, try to cover multiple angles or show movement)

Figure 1	Figure 2
Figure 3	**Figure 4**

Is this really worth making? Yes/No
What are my next steps?

Invention or Idea #: _____

Person who invented this: _____ Date: _____

What am I calling/naming it?

What does it do? (Describe what it does in 1-2 sentences):

How does it help someone or make something easier? (1-2 sentences)

Sketches: (If applicable, try to cover multiple angles or show movement)

Figure 1	Figure 2
Figure 3	Figure 4

Is this really worth making? Yes/No
What are my next steps?

Invention or Idea #: _____

Person who invented this: _____ Date: _____

What am I calling/naming it?

What does it do? (Describe what it does in 1-2 sentences):

How does it help someone or make something easier? (1-2 sentences)

Sketches: (If applicable, try to cover multiple angles or show movement)

Figure 1	Figure 2
Figure 3	**Figure 4**

Is this really worth making? Yes/No
What are my next steps?

Invention or Idea #: _____

Person who invented this: _____ Date: _____

What am I calling/naming it?

What does it do? (Describe what it does in 1-2 sentences):

How does it help someone or make something easier? (1-2 sentences)

Sketches: (If applicable, try to cover multiple angles or show movement)

Figure 1	Figure 2
Figure 3	Figure 4

Is this really worth making? Yes/No
What are my next steps?

Invention or Idea #: _____

Person who invented this: _____ Date: _____

What am I calling/naming it?

What does it do? (Describe what it does in 1-2 sentences):

How does it help someone or make something easier? (1-2 sentences)

Sketches: (If applicable, try to cover multiple angles or show movement)

Figure 1	Figure 2
Figure 3	Figure 4

Is this really worth making? Yes/No
What are my next steps?

Invention or Idea #: _____

Person who invented this: _____ Date: _____

What am I calling/naming it?

What does it do? (Describe what it does in 1-2 sentences):

How does it help someone or make something easier? (1-2 sentences)

Sketches: (If applicable, try to cover multiple angles or show movement)

Figure 1	Figure 2
Figure 3	Figure 4

Is this really worth making? Yes/No
What are my next steps?

Invention or Idea #: _____

Person who invented this: _____ Date: _____

What am I calling/naming it?

What does it do? (Describe what it does in 1-2 sentences):

How does it help someone or make something easier? (1-2 sentences)

Sketches: (If applicable, try to cover multiple angles or show movement)

Figure 1	Figure 2
Figure 3	Figure 4

Is this really worth making? Yes/No
What are my next steps?

Invention or Idea #: _____

Person who invented this: _____ Date: _____

What am I calling/naming it?

What does it do? (Describe what it does in 1-2 sentences):

How does it help someone or make something easier? (1-2 sentences)

Sketches: (If applicable, try to cover multiple angles or show movement)

Figure 1	Figure 2
Figure 3	Figure 4

Is this really worth making? Yes/No
What are my next steps?

Invention or Idea #: _____

Person who invented this: _____ Date: _____

What am I calling/naming it?

What does it do? (Describe what it does in 1-2 sentences):

How does it help someone or make something easier? (1-2 sentences)

Sketches: (If applicable, try to cover multiple angles or show movement)

Figure 1	Figure 2
Figure 3	Figure 4

Is this really worth making? Yes/No
What are my next steps?

Invention or Idea #: _____

Person who invented this: _____ Date: _____

What am I calling/naming it?

What does it do? (Describe what it does in 1-2 sentences):

How does it help someone or make something easier? (1-2 sentences)

Sketches: (If applicable, try to cover multiple angles or show movement)

Figure 1	Figure 2
Figure 3	Figure 4

Is this really worth making? Yes/No
What are my next steps?

Invention or Idea #: _____

Person who invented this: _____ Date: _____

What am I calling/naming it?

What does it do? (Describe what it does in 1-2 sentences):

How does it help someone or make something easier? (1-2 sentences)

Sketches: (If applicable, try to cover multiple angles or show movement)

Figure 1	Figure 2
Figure 3	Figure 4

Is this really worth making? Yes/No
What are my next steps?

Invention or Idea #: _____

Person who invented this: _____ Date: _____

What am I calling/naming it?

What does it do? (Describe what it does in 1-2 sentences):

How does it help someone or make something easier? (1-2 sentences)

Sketches: (If applicable, try to cover multiple angles or show movement)

Figure 1	Figure 2
Figure 3	**Figure 4**

Is this really worth making? Yes/No
What are my next steps?

Invention or Idea #: _____

Person who invented this: _____ Date: _____

What am I calling/naming it?

What does it do? (Describe what it does in 1-2 sentences):

How does it help someone or make something easier? (1-2 sentences)

Sketches: (If applicable, try to cover multiple angles or show movement)

Figure 1	Figure 2
Figure 3	Figure 4

Is this really worth making? Yes/No
What are my next steps?

www.ingramcontent.com/pod-product-compliance
Lightning Source LLC
Chambersburg PA
CBHW080832310526
45788CB00019B/3273